HEALING BECOMES A JOURNEY

(Never Lost My Praise)

THEODORE HUGHES

Associate Pastor
of Faith Church

Copyright ©2014
When A Healing Becomes A Journey/ Theodore Hughes

ISBN: 978-0-9906776-2-8

ALL RIGHTS RESERVED. This book contains material protected under International and Federal Copyright Laws and Treaties. Any unauthorized reprint or use of this material is prohibited. No part of this book may be reproduced or transmitted in any form or by any means, electronic or mechanical, including photocopying, recording, or by any information storage and retrieval system without express written permission from the author/publisher.

Printed in United States of America

DEDICATION

I dedicate this experience to my wife, Nadine, whom I have loved for many years, who at times was nurse and the push I needed to secure concrete answers from the many doctors who joined me on this journey. To my four daughters, Shekinah Draper, Shannon Davidson, Tamara Hughes, Thea Hughes, whose love and concern I will always value. To Faith Church and my Pastors Terry and Robin Bates, who were instrumental in engaging prayer groups and individuals across the United States to include me in their prayer focus.

TABLE of CONTENTS

Purpose	xi
Chapter 1 – Start Of A New Day	1
Chapter 2 – Needle Biopsy	5
Chapter 3 – Sharing My Condition	9
Chapter 4 – Bad News / Good News	15
Chapter 5 – Chemo Medications And Side Effects	27
Chapter 6 – My Salvation Testimony	39
Chapter 7 – Second Week Of Treatment	45
Chapter 8 – Third Week Of Treatment	49
Chapter 9 – Fourth Week Of Treatment	53
Chapter 10 – Fifth Week Of Treatment	59
Chapter 11 – Sixth Week Of Treatment	65
Chapter 12 – My Healing Journey Is Coming To An End	71

PURPOSE

The purpose of this testimony is to convince Christians that God does heal immediately as well as progressively. Also to realize that tough moments are a part of this earthly life. In everything that happens, **God has a purpose** that will work out for the good of those who love Him and are called according to His purpose. For all others, He uses life's challenges to help individuals realize their great need for Him and His desire to partner with them throughout life.

Romans 8:28 ~ And we know that in all things God works for the good of those who love him, who have been called according to his purpose. (NIV)

In addition the goodness of God leads a person to repentance. (to change a person's thinking).

Romans 2:4 ~ Or do you show contempt for the riches of his kindness, tolerance and patience, not realizing that God's kindness leads you toward repentance? (NIV)

For full clarity of the proof scriptures that I have selected, please read the surrounding verses and even the chapter from which the verse is quoted. I have witnessed many Christians struggle in their belief system when trouble or difficult experiences develop. It is good to know that God is our refuge and strength, a very present help in trouble.

Psalms 46:1 ~ God is our refuge and strength, an ever-present help in trouble. (NIV)

I realize that, all things being equal, no one ever hopes to start out their day with a tragedy. Yet, when difficult times come questions arise such as, "Why me?" or "What did I do wrong?" God never promised that we, as Christians, would live in some sort of bubble of protection from all hurt, harm and danger. During my early ministry, I worked with Teen Challenge in Darmstadt, Germany, and the winter weather was nothing like that of Louisiana. The clothes that I packed were sorely inadequate. One morning during prayer, I began to ask God for a winter coat. One evening we received a care package from the States. In the box was a rugged looking tweed coat. I tried it on and was surprised that it fit. I began to praise God for the coat that I considered an answer to prayer. As I paraded around thanking God, I noticed that the coat did not have any buttons. I went out that evening to do some street evangelism and periodically I would have to pull the coat together to stop the cold from coming in. That night, when we returned home, I began to wonder about the buttons. I went to the prayer room to pray. After a time of thanking God for His goodness, grace and mercy, I asked Him a question that pressed heavily on my mind, **"Lord, why did you give me a coat without any buttons?"** This may sound silly, even unappreciative of the coat, but for me, I was convinced that God could do anything and that He always has my best interest in mind. After two or three days of bringing this matter about the buttons before God, I finally received an answer. He said to my mind, **"It is necessary for your sake that I leave you opportunities to come to Me again."** I learned that God will not put us in a position that would cause us to not need Him anymore. I began to pray for buttons for my coat. One of our ministry team noticed that I did not have any buttons on my coat. She indicated that she had a sowing kit and extra buttons. God said that He would never leave us or forsake us, especially during the tough times of life. No one really knows how they will react or respond in a time of crisis. Even though many people rehearse possible reactions to a difficulty or tragedy, our reaction to that incident is still uncertain on multiple levels. This concept is implied in the Gospel of Mark and the solution is given to the believer in the scripture below.

Mark 13:10-11 ~ "10 And the gospel must first be published among all nations. 11 But when they shall lead you, and deliver you up, take no thought beforehand what ye shall speak, neither do ye premeditate: but whatsoever shall be given you in that hour, that speak ye: for it is not ye that speak, but the Holy Ghost." (KJV)

God is in control of everything that occurs and His purpose is to develop integrity, character, strength, trustworthiness, faith, compassion, love, a sense of purpose, purity or righteousness and every good principle that leads to His glorification, which is in our best interest. If mankind is left to his/her own devices the end result without God deteriorates into a river of selfishness (concerned excessively or exclusively with oneself).

Below are some scriptures' principles that help me to understand "**the why**" in the tough moments that Christians experience in this life.

1 Samuel 1:5-7 ~ "5 But to Hannah he would give a double portion, for he loved Hannah, **although the Lord**

had closed her womb. 6 And her rival also provoked her severely, to make her miserable, because the Lord had closed her womb. 7 So it was, year by year, when she went up to the house of the Lord, that she provoked her; therefore she wept and did not eat." (NKJV)

1 Samuel 1:9-15 ~ "9 So Hannah arose after they had finished eating and drinking in Shiloh. Now Eli the priest was sitting on the seat by the doorpost of the tabernacle of the Lord. 10 And **she was in bitterness of soul**, and prayed to the Lord and wept in anguish. 11 Then she made a vow and said, "O Lord of hosts, if You will indeed look on the affliction of Your maidservant and remember me, and not forget Your maidservant, but will give Your maidservant a male child, then I will give him to the Lord all the days of his life, and no razor shall come upon his head." 12 And it happened, as she **continued praying** before the Lord, that Eli watched her mouth. 13 Now Hannah spoke in her heart; only her lips moved, but her voice was not heard. Therefore Eli thought she was drunk. 14 So Eli said to her, "How long will you be drunk? Put your wine away from you!" 15 But Hannah answered and said, "No, my lord, **I am a woman of sorrowful spirit. I have drunk neither wine nor intoxicating drink, but have poured out my soul before the Lord**." (NKJV)

This is a tough moment for Hannah. It was certainly out of her control to guarantee that she would get pregnant. The harassment of her contemporary, Peninnah, for not being able to conceive, the social stigma about not being able to have a child, and her desire to have a child pushed Hannah to a breaking point that only God could mend.

Ecclesiastes 9:11 ~ "11 I have seen something else under the sun: The race is not to the swift or the battle to the strong, nor does food come to the wise or wealth to the brilliant or favor to the learned; **but time and chance happen to them all**." (NIV)

Mankind has this great ability, in most cases, to conceal, hide or cover up the pain of dealing with trouble. When it comes to revealing the mess we find ourselves in we are strongly secretive. I am not saying that we should open the door of our difficulty to everyone that passes by, but simply emphasize the fact that no one is excluded from the tough moments of life.

Isaiah 59:19 - "19 So shall they fear the name of the Lord from the west, and his glory from the rising of the sun. **When the enemy shall come in like a flood**, the Spirit of the Lord shall lift up a standard against him." (KJV)

Note the word, WHEN, denoting inevitability. Regardless of how we seek to shelter ourselves from tough times, they will come and we must rely on God to help us.

John 10:10 - "10 **The thief cometh** not, but for to steal, and to kill, and to destroy: I am come that they might have life, and that they might have it more abundantly." (KJV)

John 16:33 - "33 These things I have spoken unto you, that in me ye might have peace. **In the world ye shall have tribulation**: but be of good cheer; I have overcome the world." (KJV) Jesus uses the word, SHALL, again denoting inevitability. God allows stuff to happen to reveal to us the areas in our Christian journey that need attention and to point us to His grace and mercy when the unexpected happens.

John 15:19-21 ~ "19 If you belonged to the world, it would love you as its own. As it is, you do not belong to the world, but I have chosen you out of the world. **That is why the world hates you**. 20 Remember the words I spoke to you: 'No servant is greater than his master.' **If they persecuted me, they will persecute you also**. If they obeyed my teaching, they will obey yours also. 21 They will treat you this way because of my name, for they do not know the One who sent me." (NIV)

Acts 14:19-22 ~ "19 Then Jews from Antioch and Iconium came there; and having persuaded the multitudes, **they stoned Paul and dragged him out of the city**, supposing him to be dead. 20 However, when the disciples gathered around him, he rose up and went into the city. And the next day he departed with Barnabas to Derbe. Strengthening the Converts. 21 And when they had preached the gospel to that city and made many disciples, they returned to Lystra, Iconium, and Antioch, 22 strengthening the souls of the disciples, exhorting them to continue in the faith, and saying, "We must through many tribulations enter the kingdom of God." (NKJV)

1 Peter 5:8-9 ~ "8 Be self-controlled and alert. **Your enemy the devil prowls around like a roaring lion looking for someone to devour**. 9 Resist him, standing firm in the faith, because you know that your brothers throughout the world are undergoing the same kind of sufferings." (NIV)

Romans 8:36-37 ~ "36 As it is written: "**For your sake we face death all day long**; we are considered as sheep to be slaughtered." 37 No, in all these things we are more than conquerors through him who loved us." (NIV)

2 Corinthians 7:4 ~ "4 I have great confidence in you; I take great pride in you. I am greatly encouraged; **in all our troubles** my joy knows no bounds." (NIV)

1 Thessalonians 3:4 ~ "4 In fact, when we were with you, **we kept telling you that we would be persecuted.** And it turned out that way, as you well know." (NIV)

2 Timothy 3:12 ~ "12 In fact, everyone who wants to live a godly life in Christ Jesus **will be persecuted**," (NIV)

Hebrews 11:24-26 ~ "24 By faith Moses, when he had grown up, refused to be known as the son of Pharaoh's daughter. 25 **He chose to be mistreated along with the people of God** rather than to enjoy the pleasures of sin for a short time. 26 **He regarded disgrace for the sake of Christ** as of greater value than the treasures of Egypt, because he was looking ahead to his reward." (NIV)

Matthew 23:34 ~ "34 Therefore, indeed, **I send you prophets, wise men, and scribes: some of them you will kill and crucify**, and some of them you will scourge in your synagogues and persecute from city to city." (NKJV)

Below is a list of individuals from the scriptures who either were sick, beaten, killed and imprisoned while serving God.

Genesis 39:20-21 ~ "20 Then **Joseph's** master took him and put him into the prison, a place where the king's prisoners were confined. And he was there in the prison. 21 But the Lord was with Joseph and showed him mercy, and He gave him favor in the sight of the keeper of the prison." (NKJV)

Daniel 6:16 ~ "16 Then the king commanded, and they brought **Daniel**, and cast him into the den of lions. Now the king spake and said unto Daniel, Thy God whom thou servest continually, he will deliver thee." (KJV)

Daniel 3:22-25 ~ "22 Therefore because the king's commandment was urgent, and the furnace exceeding hot, the flame of the fire slew those men that took up **Shadrach, Meshach, and Abed-nego.** 23 And these three men, Shadrach, Meshach, and Abed-nego, fell down bound into the midst of the burning fiery furnace. 24 Then Nebuchadnezzar the king was astonied, and rose up in haste, and spake, and said unto his counsellors, Did not we cast three men bound into the midst of the fire? They answered and said unto the king, True, O king. 25 He answered and said, Lo, I see four men loose, walking in the midst of the fire, and they have no hurt; and the form of the fourth is like the Son of God." (KJV)

Matthew 7:24-25 ~ "24 Therefore whosoever heareth these sayings of mine, and doeth them, I will liken him unto a wise man, which built his house upon a rock: 25 And the **rain descended**, and the **floods came**, and the winds blew, and beat upon that house; and it fell not: for it was founded upon a rock." (KJV)

Matthew 11:2-3 ~ "2 And when **John** had heard **in prison** about the works of Christ, he sent two of his disciples. 3 and said to Him, 'Are You the Coming One, or do we look for another?' " (NKJV)

Matthew 27:26 ~ "26 Then he released Barabbas to them. But he had **Jesus** flogged, and handed him over to be crucified." (NIV)

Mark 6:25-27 ~ "25 Immediately she came in with haste to the king and asked, saying, 'I want you to give me at once **the head of John the Baptist on a platter**'. 26 And the king was exceedingly sorry; yet, because of the oaths and because of those who sat with him, he did not want to refuse her. 27 Immediately the king sent an executioner and commanded his head to be brought. **And he went and beheaded him in prison**," (NKJV)

Acts 5:17-20 ~ "17 Then the high priest rose up, and all those who were with him (which is the sect of the Sadducees), and they were filled with indignation, 18 and laid their hands on the **apostles** and put them in the common prison. 19 But at night an angel of the Lord opened the prison doors and brought them out, and said, 20 "Go, stand in the temple and speak to the people all the words of this life." (NKJV)

Acts 12:5-7 ~ "5 **Peter** was therefore kept in prison, but constant prayer was offered to God for him by the church. 6 And when Herod was about to bring him out, that night Peter was sleeping, bound with two chains between two soldiers; and the guards before the door were keeping the prison. 7 Now behold, an angel of the Lord stood by him, and a light shone in the prison; and he struck Peter on the side and raised him up, saying, 'Arise quickly!' And his chains fell off his hands." (NKJV)

Acts 14:19-20 ~ "19 Then some Jews came from Antioch and Iconium and won the crowd over. They stoned **Paul** and dragged him outside the city, thinking he was dead. 20 But after the disciples had gathered around him, he got up and went back into the city. The next day he and Barnabas left for Derbe." (NIV)

Acts 16:19; 22-26 ~ "19 But when her masters saw that their hope of profit was gone, they seized Paul and **Silas** and dragged them into the marketplace to the authorities. 22 Then the multitude rose up together against them; and the magistrates tore off their clothes and commanded them to be beaten with rods. 23 And when they had laid many stripes on them, they threw them into prison, commanding the jailer to keep them securely. 24 Having received such a charge, he put them into the inner prison and fastened their feet in the stocks. 25 But at midnight Paul and Silas were praying and singing hymns to God, and the prisoners were listening to them. 26 Suddenly there was a great earthquake, so that the foundations of the prison were shaken; and immediately all the doors were opened and everyone's chains were loosed." (NKJV)

2 Corinthians 11:23-27 ~ Apostle Paul was following God's plan to reach his generation with a determination to preach the gospel to different people groups who have never experienced the Good News of Jesus Christ. Even though Paul was doing God's will, he experienced some very difficult challenges listed below. "23 Are they servants of Christ? (I am out of my mind to talk like this.) I am more. I have worked much harder, **been in prison more frequently**, been **flogged** more severely, and been **exposed to death** again and again. 24 **Five times** I received from the Jews the **forty lashes** minus one. 25 Three times I was **beaten with rods**, once I was **stoned**, three times I was **shipwrecked**, I spent a night and a day in the open sea, 26 I have been constantly on the move. I have been **in danger from rivers, in danger from bandits, in danger from my own countrymen, in danger from Gentiles; in danger in the city, in danger in the country, in**

danger at sea; and in danger from false brothers. 27 I have labored and toiled and have often **gone without sleep**; I have known **hunger** and **thirst** and have often gone **without food**; I have been **cold** and **naked**." (NIV)

Philippians 2:25-27 – "25 Yet I supposed it necessary to send to you **Epaphroditus**, my brother, and companion in labour, and fellowsoldier, but your messenger, and he that ministered to my wants. 26 For he longed after you all, and was full of heaviness, **because that ye had heard that he had been sick**. 27 For indeed he was sick nigh unto death: but God had mercy on him; and not on him only, but on me also, lest I should have sorrow upon sorrow." (KJV)

Hebrews 11:35-38 – "35 Women received back their dead, raised to life again. **Others** were tortured and refused to be released, so that they might gain a better resurrection. 36 **Some** faced jeers and flogging, while still **others** were chained and put in prison. 37 They were **stoned**; they were **sawed in two**; they **were put to death by the sword**. They went about in sheepskins and goatskins, destitute, persecuted and mistreated — 38 the world was not worthy of them. **They wandered** in deserts and mountains, and in caves and holes in the ground." (NIV)

1 Corinthians 4:8-13 – "8 Already you have all you want! Already you have become rich! You have become kings — and that without us! How I wish that you really had become kings so that we might be kings with you! 9 For it seems to me that God has put us **apostles** on **display** at the end of the procession, like men condemned to die in the arena. We have **been made a spectacle** to the whole universe, to angels as well as to men. 10 We are fools for Christ, but you are so wise in Christ! We are weak, but you are strong! You are honored, we are dishonored! 11 **To this very hour** we go hungry and thirsty, we are in rags, we are brutally treated, we are homeless. 12 We work hard with our own hands. When we are cursed, we bless; when we are persecuted, we endure it; 13 when we are slandered, we answer kindly. Up to this moment we have become the scum of the earth, the refuse of the world." (NIV)

In the above scriptures' passages, there is no mention of disdain, complaining, or murmuring, but a desire to continue to share the gospel in spite of life's hardships and resistances by some people groups. From these scriptures I drew strength along with the prayers of many Christians and by the grace of God that was able to endure my journey to a complete healing.

When I received the news that I had malignant lymphoma, I along with many others, asked God to remove this tumor immediately. Instead, my healing became a journey that presented me with many real life opportunities to let doctors, nurses, other Christians and patients know that the love of God is real; some were challenged to re-examine their faith in God through Jesus Christ. I asked those who were of eastern religions, "How do you say 'God' in your language?" When they responded, it gave me an opportunity to share the love of God with them. It is true that God has the ability to shield Christians from all adversity. The Scriptures indicate that He does not shield us on purpose because of another one of His principles located in the book of Isaiah.

Isaiah 55:8-9 ~ "8 For my thoughts are not your thoughts, neither are your ways my ways, saith the Lord. 9 For as the heavens are higher than the earth, so are my ways higher than your ways, and my thoughts than your thoughts." (KJV)

It is obvious that God sees farther, knows everything, is everywhere and is all powerful. Jesus being the master teacher and Earth being his classroom, presented principles, concepts and insights of what is happening in Heaven that can be reproduced on Earth. When we analyze the story of Lazarus, we can clearly see that Jesus allowed Lazarus to die to create a teaching moment for the disciples and to demonstrate His power to resurrect someone who is clearly dead by local cultural standards.

John 11:1-6; 11-15 – "11 Now a certain man was sick, Lazarus of Bethany, the town of Mary and her sister Martha. 2 It was that Mary who anointed the Lord with fragrant oil and wiped His feet with her hair, whose brother Lazarus was sick. 3 Therefore the sisters sent to Him, saying, 'Lord, behold, he whom You love is sick.' " 4 When Jesus heard that, He said, 'This sickness is not unto death, but for the glory of God, that the Son of God may be glorified through it.' 5 Now Jesus loved Martha and her sister and Lazarus. 6 So, when He heard that he was sick, He stayed two more days in the place where He was.

11 These things He said, and after that He said to them, 'Our friend Lazarus sleeps, but I go that I may wake him up.' 12 Then His disciples said, 'Lord, if he sleeps he will get well.' 13 However, Jesus spoke of his death, but they thought that He was speaking about taking rest in sleep. 14 Then Jesus said to them plainly, 'Lazarus is dead. 15 And I am glad for your sakes that I was not there, that you may believe. Nevertheless let us go to him'." (NKJV)

John 11:21-26 ~ "21 Now Martha said to Jesus, 'Lord, if You had been here, my brother would not have died. 22 But even now I know that whatever You ask of God, God will give You." 23 Jesus said to her, 'Your brother will rise again.' 24 Martha said to Him, 'I know that he will rise again in the resurrection at the last day.' 25 Jesus said to her, "I am the resurrection and the life. He who believes in Me, though he may die, he shall live. 26 And whoever lives and believes in Me shall never die. Do you believe this?" (NJKV)

John 11:43-44 ~ "43 Now when He had said these things, He cried with a loud voice, 'Lazarus, come forth!' 44 And he who had died came out bound hand and foot with grave clothes, and his face was wrapped with a cloth. Jesus said to them, 'Loose him, and let him go.' (NJKV)

Isaiah 46:9-10 ~ "9 Remember the former things of old: for I am God, and there is none else; I am God, and there is none like me, 10 Declaring the end from the beginning, and from ancient times the things that are not yet done, saying, My counsel shall stand, and I will do all my pleasure:" (KJV)

God has a way of using every situation, incident and circumstance as a teaching tool to help mankind understand that He is God and that He has our best interest at heart. **The downside of learning from the heart of God is our failure to grasp immediately what God is trying to teach us**. I have seen individuals who are constantly making bad choices and subsequently suffer from the consequences. God simply steps in and uses each circumstance, situation and incident to try and draw people close to His heart. As I journeyed to a complete healing, what I experienced will be of great benefit to you directly or indirectly. If you would share my journey to a healing, with someone who is asking the questions, "Lord Why Me? Why Now? What have I done wrong? Will I survive this? Will the treatments work?' I will deeply appreciate it. My purpose in writing this book is to help the next person whose healing becomes a journey, to move beyond the process and take comfort in the fact that God will journey with them. When the hospital hallways become quiet, when friends and family return to their homes, when all you have is the sound of the IV pump, the groans of another patient and your thoughts, you can have this inner peace knowing that you are not alone.

CHAPTER ONE
Start of a New Day

During the first week of March, 2013, I woke up and began to prepare myself for another day of serving the Lord by serving His people. I quoted **Psalms 118:24** (KJV), "This is the day which the LORD hath made; we will rejoice and be glad in it." I always like to emphasize the phrase "will rejoice" and "be glad." **Will** is called upon to express desire, choice, consent, habitual action or natural tendency. **Be** stresses reality or actuality, identity with or same class. For a Christian to rejoice in God is not some foreign or strange act, nor is it accidental or happen stance. To rejoice in God is an act of appreciation, gratitude and a reminder that all that we are or ever hope to be starts and ends with Him. I lathered my face and began to shave. Afterwards I applied some after shave lotion only to discover a lump under my lift jaw. I made a mental note to call my primary care physician, Dr. Legg-Jack, of the Veteran's North May Clinic, about mid-morning. When I telephoned, a nurse answered. I explained to her what I had discovered. She said that she would tell the doctor and that I would be contacted. Around 3:30PM the nurse said that Dr. Legg-Jack suspects infection in my lymph node. I was told to go to the downtown Veterans Administration Hospital Pharmacy and pick up a supply of antibiotics. I began to take the antibiotics immediately. After several days, I noticed that the lump was getting larger. I continued to take the antibiotics until they were all gone. I called Dr. Legg-Jack and scheduled an appointment with him for further evaluation. As he examined me, he asked, "Are you experiencing any pain?" I said, "None." He said, "That's not good."

I had always associated no pain as a good thing. Dr. Legg-Jack said that he would schedule a biopsy of the lump and that I would be contacted by telephone concerning the date and time. When scheduling a procedure through the Veteran Administration Hospital System delays are part of the approval process. While waiting for the call to schedule a biopsy, I let my wife, Nadine, examine the lump that was becoming quite noticeable. After she looked at the lump, she recommended that I get a second opinion. I went to Canadian Valley Hospital to secure an appointment with a primary care doctor assigned to our family through United Health Care. I approached the desk with confidence, thinking that I would receive immediate care. The person behind the desk was very kind. She contacted the doctor, who said that I had not been seen for a long time and must be treated as a new patient. That did not pose a problem to me. I was told that I needed to fill out a series of paper work to establish my medical history. The shocker was that the next opening for new patients was three weeks to a month out. This was close to the time that my biopsy was scheduled. **I refused to give in to the "O my God look what is happening to me mindset!"** I contacted Deaconess Hospital. I was told that they have no Oncology Department and would follow the same procedures as Dr. Legg-Jack, who was scheduling me for a biopsy. By the way Dr. Legg-Jack is a Christian from Ghana West Africa. "Also the doctor said to let him know of my progress. **God has been good to me.** During this time Melissa Kennedy gave my wife and me some great advice about becoming more aggressive in getting medical attention. I was a few days out from my appointment when it became very apparent to my Christian friends, family and me that the lump on the left side of my face looked serious. My awareness level was high but my determination to maintain a confidence and hope in God's ability to heal me was higher.

Theodore Hughes

CHAPTER TWO
Needle Biopsy

I shared with our Church Staff that I was scheduled for a Needle Biopsy. Upon arriving at the Veterans Hospital, I checked in and within moments was taken to a room just off of the hallway. I was told to lie down on the examination bed. The doctor began to insert a needle into the tumor. Because the word had spread about my biopsy, Rick Newby and Brian Shirey came to the hospital and boldly walked into the examination room.

I was very happy to see them. My mind went to the scripture in **Ecclesiastes 4:9-10** (KJV) "Two are better than one; because they have a good reward for their labor. For if they fall, the one will lift up his fellow: but woe to him that is alone when he falleth; for he hath not another to help him up." Even though I was willing to go through the biopsy alone, Rick and Brian were added strength that I needed. They continued to talk to me, using words of encouragement and affirming the healing power of our God through Jesus Christ. **God has been good to me.** I asked the doctor if he could tell me if the biopsy was malignant or benign. He said that he would need to take more samples, which he did. After several minutes and multiple needle pricks, the doctor said that I had a malignant lymphoma. I thanked the doctor for letting me know. He placed a bandage on my jaw and said to follow up with my primary care doctor. **During this process, the doctor told Rick that I should take this matter more seriously.** His observation was that I did not seem discouraged or defeated, but upbeat in my demeanor. In my thinking, falling on the floor in a ball of pity was not going to change my condition, so I decided not to change my confidence in God's ability to work a miracle and to rejoice in the same in advance. As Rick, Brian and I left the room, we joined hands and prayed for several minutes and quoted scriptures concerning healing. We continued our conversation as we walked across the parking lot to my truck. After talking for some time we concluded that God will help us through this tough moment. Throughout this process, I was not going to let this diagnosis change my praise to God and my caring for His people. I became more determined not to lose my Praise.

Over the years of reading the book of Job, I am very impressed at the attitude he displayed. This kind of statement is developed from sharing continuous and close relations. To be in a place, of which, you know that God is always working on your behalf regardless of the situation is a very good place.

Job 1:21-22 ~ 21 And said, Naked came I out of my mother's womb, and naked shall I return thither: **the Lord gave, and the Lord hath taken away; blessed be the name of the Lord. 22 In all this Job sinned not, nor charged God foolishly.** (KJV)

Theodore Hughes

CHAPTER THREE
Sharing My Condition

While driving back to the office, I called Pastor Bates to inform him of my diagnosis. After he shared some encouraging words and a declaration that he would stand with me throughout this journey, my thoughts turned to my family. How will they receive this information? What will their questions be?

I called Dr. Legg-Jack and informed him of the diagnosis. He immediately began working on scheduling me for a CAT SCAN - a method of producing a three-dimensional image of the internal structures of a solid object (as the human body or the earth) by the observation and recording of the differences in the effects on the passage of waves of energy impinging on those structures. Because the scheduling of the CAT SCAN was almost three weeks out, I went to Access Medical to see if they could determine the spread of the Cancer. They used ultra sound which revealed lesions (An abnormal change in structure of an organ or part due to injury or disease). They could not determine the spread of the cancer, but simply recommended that I get a CAT SCAN. I had to settle myself down and recommit myself to the hands of my Heavenly Father. I remembered the words of Jesus in the Garden of Gethsemane, in particular, "Not my will but thy will be done."

Matthew 26:36-39 ~ "36 Then cometh Jesus with them unto a place called Gethsemane, and saith unto the disciples, Sit ye here, while I go and pray yonder. 37 And he took with him Peter and the two sons of Zebedee, and began to be sorrowful and very heavy. 38 Then saith he unto them, My soul is exceeding sorrowful, even unto death: tarry ye here, and watch with me. 39 And he went a little further, and fell on his face, and prayed, saying, **O my Father, if it be possible, let this cup pass from me: nevertheless not as I will, but as thou wilt**." (KJV)

Matthew 26:42 ~ "42 He went away again the second time, and prayed, saying, **O my Father, if this cup may not pass away from me, except I drink it, thy will be done**." (KJV)

While I was at home waiting for my wife, Nadine, to arrive from work, I began to think of the strong life-exiting testimonies of Christian friends, Church members and acquaintances, I have had the honor of being with in their final hours, as God called them from this Earth to their new home in Heaven. Now here I was, in a position that I had never been before, facing an illness with the potential of ending my life on Earth. I thought, "What will my response be? What do I do as I face the possibility of dying?" It is amazing how much information the mind can process in a short time period. At this point I was still trying to frame the words for living to my wife when she arrived and, at the same time, rejoice that I might be seeing Jesus face to face. Paul experienced this kind of emotion when dealing with the Philippian Church.

Philippians 1:23-24 ~ "23 **For I am in a strait betwixt two, having a desire to depart, and to be with Christ; which is far better** 24 Nevertheless to abide in the flesh is more needful for you. 25 And having this confidence, I know that I shall abide and continue with you all for your furtherance and joy of faith; 26 That your rejoicing may be more abundant in Jesus Christ for me by my coming to you again." (KJV)

I heard the garage door opening, which meant that my wife, Nadine, had arrived. I remained seated on the sofa until she came into the kitchen area. We greeted each other with our normal kiss. I decided to weigh right in and tell her, with balanced emotions, exactly what the doctors told me. This I think helped her to process the information with hope and strength. Then it was time to tell my mother and my four daughters, Shekinah, Shannon, Tamara, and Thea.

Theodore Hughes

My sister, Elizabeth Harvey, was diagnosed with terminal cancer and given two weeks to live, and subsequently passed. It is more natural for a child to outlive the parent, than for a parent to outlive the child. My Pastor and friend, Terry Bates, and I observed my mother at my sister's funeral, and listened to her words, "I never thought that I would be attending my child's funeral." Now I had the unpleasant task of telling my mother, Josephine Mildred Hughes, that I had malignant lymphoma. Even though my wife, daughters and mother displayed strong emotional feelings, my manner of communicating helped them to process the information. The possibility of enduring the death of a child, husband and dad is a very serious matter.

> *"You never know how strong you are until being strong is your only choice."*
>
> ~ Bob Morley

During the early days of my journey to a complete healing, my wife, Nadine and I decided to visit some long-time friends, Floyd and Saundra Burleson, in Cedar Hill, Texas. We were thinking that the trip to Texas might offer some reprieve from the daily reminder of the cancer in my body. There were times we would discuss an event that we enjoyed together. Afterwards we would drift into long periods of silence. As I slipped into the automatic driving mode, I began to ask myself questions. Could this be our last trip together? After so many years of being together, how do you say goodbye? How do I explain the tumor on the left side of my face to the Burleson's? What would be their reactions? When we arrived, there were the usual warm embraces and sentiments. As we settled in around some refreshments, Floyd began to tell me about his latest diagnosis. His primary care doctor determined that he, Floyd, had prostate cancer. We laughed and talked about our similarities; our birthdays, style of clothes, temperaments and many other qualities were identical. Now we both are diagnosed with cancer. After discussing how we are going to trust God for a complete healing and maintain a good attitude throughout the process, we committed ourselves to God's purpose and a two-man domino tournament. This was good therapy for both of us. The mental stress of being diagnosed with cancer and the varying outcomes dissolved for the next four hours. As we prepared to return to Oklahoma, Floyd, Saundra, my wife, Nadine and I prayed for a miracle of healing for Floyd and then for me.

Theodore Hughes

CHAPTER FOUR
Bad News / Good News

There are six Biblical Principles that helped me communicate my health to my family as presented by the doctors.

1. **God's Peace - Isaiah 26:3; John 14:27**
2. **God's Patience - Hebrews 10:36**
3. **God's Power - Acts 1:8**
4. **God's Presence - Deuteronomy 31:6**
5. **God's Grace - James 4:6**
6. **God's Generosity - Psalms 115:14**

As I thought about my health, I actually began to get very happy. I am in a **WIN/WIN** situation. If God takes me to Heaven I WIN. If He decides to leave me one Earth for a little while longer, I WIN.

There are three questions that I asked myself during this journey.

1. **What is God saying through this?**
2. **What lessons are to be learned?**
3. **What can I do to help?**

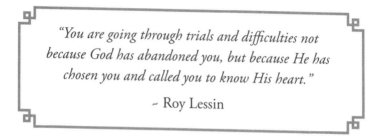

"You are going through trials and difficulties not because God has abandoned you, but because He has chosen you and called you to know His heart."

~ Roy Lessin

I received a call from the Veterans Administration Hospital stating that I was scheduled to meet with Dr. Parekh at the VA Cancer Center on a Tuesday. My wife, Nadine, and Pastor Bates accompanied me for this initial consultation. After Dr. Parekh asked me to clarify why I was meeting with her, she said that even though malignant lymphoma was the initial diagnosis, we must realize that there are many different strains of lymphoma. Then she began to outline the possible steps that I would be facing as I journeyed to complete healing, including, a bone marrow biopsy, tumor site biopsy, possible stem cell transplant, blood analysis and six treatments of chemotherapy, with each treatment lasting five days with a two week recovery between each treatment. As Dr. Parekh was outlining the process, Pastor Bates, Nadine and I were allowed to ask questions and get farther clarifications. It was during the month of March 2013 that all of this began to come to a head. Also during this time Pastor Bates scheduled an appreciation ceremony for Nadine and me for fifteen years of faithful and loyal service at Faith Church. While standing on the churches' platform, I was very much aware of the tumor, that was very pronounced, on the left side of my face.

During the Sunday morning service Pastor Bates called for the elders of the church and invited the entire Faith Family to join in prayer for my healing.

This was the beginning of the prayer vigil that would sustain my family and me throughout this healing process. As a matter of fact, I have never experienced the focused prayer of so many people praying for my family and me in my forty years of ministry service. I was scheduled for a series of biopsies to determine the kind of lymphoma and its spread. The first was of my bone marrow. The procedure was scheduled for fifteen minutes. **God has been good to me.** When I arrived at the Veterans Hospital, I was taken to a small room with a single bed, counter and chair. Jamie Shirey, who came to support my wife, Nadine, waited in a small waiting area, where a couple of chairs were placed.

After some prep work by the nurse and Dr. Lamb, I was told to lie face down on the narrow bed. After farther prep work on me, Dr. Lamb began. He was gracious enough to talk me through each phase of the procedure in extracting a sampling of my bone marrow. The numbing medicine was inserted at the sight and all the way to the surface of my upper hip bone. What was scheduled as a fifteen minute procedure slowly became a one hour and five minute ordeal. It turned out that my hip bone is very hard, which is not a bad thing. But in regards to extracting bone marrow, this can be very challenging to a doctor. Dr. Lamb pushed as hard as he could within reason. I felt myself being pushed into the mattress and I could hear a sawing sound as the doctor was doing his best to make this procedure as patient friendly as possible. As I was praising God in my mind, Dr. Lamb said that he was about to break through the surface of my hip bone. He counted one, two, and three then suddenly there was a moment or two of sharp pain and a soft release of pressure sensation. He began to extract my bone marrow, which is a tissue that occupies the cavities of most bones and occurs in two forms: One type is yellowish and is made up of fat cells, which is found especially in the cavities of long bones. Another type is reddish, and is the main place for blood cell formation. Dr. Lamb said that he could not get enough bone marrow and a section of bone from this site. **God has been good to me!** He pulled out his instruments and began to prep another area inches west of the first site. As he began to cut into my hipbone again, the instrument slipped eastward into the first hole, tearing through the flesh between. Dr. Lamb pulled back his instrument and with greater pressure pushed into the second hole only to have the instrument to slip northward. I continued to praise God regardless of the pain. He was doing the best that he could but my hipbone was very difficult because of its hardness. Dr. Lamb decided to stop the procedure and settle for the small amount of bone and bone marrow collected from the first site. He did not want to subject me to any more traumas. He said, "It is your choice if you want to try the left hip." I said, "since we are here let's go for it." As he prepared the site, I clutched the pillow under my head and prayed **Matthew 6:9-13 (NKJV), "Our Father in heaven, Hallowed be Your name. Your Kingdom come. Your will be done on earth as it is in heaven. Give us this day our daily bread. And forgive us our debts, as we forgive our debtors. And do not lead us into temptation, but deliver us from the evil one. For Yours is the kingdom and the power and the glory forever. Amen."** I was not going to let this procedure stop my praise, because **God has been good to me**. After some time, Dr. Lamb said that he had gotten enough bone and bone marrow for the laboratory. "Hallelujah!" was my reply. I was told to lie flat on my back for one hour. After the hour passed, I prepared myself to leave the room. I found that standing and walking was very difficult, but I kept this to myself. Jamie had to go back to the office to take care of a matter. My wife, Nadine, and I joined hands as we walked out of the hospital. About a week later, we were told that there was no cancer in my bone marrow. Still the doctors were not sure of the strain of cancer that was still growing under my left jaw. I continued to go to the office, teach, counsel and attend Sunday church services with joy. I made up my mind that I was not going to let cancer rob me of my praise because **God has been good to me**. I was told by telephone that a PET SCAN (a three-dimensional image of the internal structure of an object) was ordered for my head and that I was to arrive at the Veterans Hospital thirty minutes early for this procedure. The first PET SCAN revealed that the tumor was located in my left jaw area only. But it did not tell what kind of tumor was there. After about a week and a half, I was asked to report to the Veterans Hospital for a Core Biopsy. I had no idea what this procedure entailed. When I arrived, I was told to sit in a special examination chair. Moments later, the doctor came in with patient consent forms. After he explained the procedures, danger and its purpose, I signed the forms. I looked at the desk where instruments for this procedure lay. There was a needle-like tool that seemed to be about a foot long. The doctor said that he could only numb the surface area of my jaw where a small cut would be placed to insert the long needle that was lying on the desk. The doctor explained that he could not do anything about the pain that I might experience when he pushed the needle into the tumor. This statement was not something that I wanted to hear. I was told to sit very straight and not to move my head. The doctor cleaned my skin, and applied the numbing agent. After a few minutes, I saw the doctor reach for the surgical knife. I began to pray and praise God for His goodness and mercy. I could feel the pressure of the cut followed by the insertion of the needle like tool. As he pushed the tool into my jaw, I was thinking that the tool was longer than the depth of my jaw. In short, the needle-like tool could easily exit the back of my jaw because of its length. After inserting the tool three times into the tumor, the doctor said that he had enough pieces to send to the lab. Instead of a surgical stitch, the doctor decided to use skin glue to close the cut. After waiting another week for a report and subsequent treatment, I was told that a larger piece of the tumor was needed. To accomplish this, I was scheduled for surgery at the Veterans Hospital eight days after the core biopsy. Nadine, drove me to the hospital. Shortly after arriving, I went through the preliminary steps for surgery. Jamie Shirey, Michael Murphy and Henry Amador joined my wife and daughters as we waited for the surgeon and the anesthesiologist to give me the pre-surgery talk, along with a time of questioning and answering. My baby daughter, Thea, asked everyone present for the privilege of having some private time with me before my surgery, a moment I will cherish. Because the tumor was so large, I experienced difficulty in bending or turning my neck to the left. At my request the surgeon biopsied the lower half of the tumor, which I thought would allow more mobility.

After the surgery was over, I woke up and noticed that the nurses were concerned about my blood pressure. Within an hour my blood pressure was stable enough for me to be sent home. During this process I could not lift my head. I was extremely dizzy and nauseated. **God is good to me**. When we were told that no nurse was available to take me to my vehicle, Pastor Bates, who was waiting with my family while I was in surgery, pushed my wheel chair. I was so dizzy that I could not stand on my own. Pastor Bates lifted me and helped me to get into the passenger side of my truck.

While we were stopped at the signal light on Lincoln Street traveling south, I emptied the contents of my stomach onto the street, resulting in me feeling much better.

Pastors Terry and Robin Bates

The biopsy was sent to a lab that was not directly connected to OU Medical Center. The conclusion was that I had Burkitt's Lymphoma. Burkitt's Lymphoma, is a very rare form of cancer with only about 300 new cases a year in the United States. Burkitt's Lymphoma, rare in most of the world, is the most common childhood cancer in Central Africa, and is one of the most aggressive of all human cancers. Burkitt's Lymphoma has a history of developing and rupturing only to start the process again.

Dr. Parekh scheduled me for a second PET scan, which revealed that cancer was under my left lower jaw, just behind my left collarbone and on both sides of my chest. A couple of days later I was notified by phone that I was to be admitted into the VA hospital immediately for treatment. Within a few hours of being admitted a nurse from OU Medical Center came in and explained that I would need to have a PICC Line inserted to administer the chemo that I was to receive to kill the cancer in my body. I was told to lie flat on my back with my left arm just above shoulder level. The PICC line specialist created a sterile field under my right shoulder and used, as she described, an ultra sound machine to guide her as she inserted a flexible tube into my vein. The line entered under my right arm, and into my heart. I felt like the PICC line was being placed in an uncomfortable position under my arm. I asked the specialist if she could route the line on the front side of my shoulder. She tried twice. The vein in that area started out large and then narrowed, causing increasing pain as the line was being threaded through. I was cautioned not to move to avoid puncturing my vein. The Specialist retracted the line and proceeded to prep my under arm. After another incision, the line was successfully threaded into a vein under my arm, across my chest and down into my heart. When she finished, I had about three inches of tubing hanging from under my arm with three ports, called a triple lumen. Another nurse came in and attached a saline bag from the IV pole near my bed. Three doctors visited me and explained that I would undergo six chemo treatments, each lasting five days, and six lumbar punctures with a two week break between treatments. They also explained that the cancer treatment and medication must be timely and that monitoring of my vital signs would be critical.

I later realized that the Oncology doctors and some of the nurses were walking from OU Medical Center to the VA Hospital and that a reduced nursing staff covered the overnight shifts at the VA Hospital. I decided to be discharged from the VA Hospital and be admitted into OU Medical Center, which was in my best interest medically. **God has been good to me.** About one hour after being assigned to a room at OU Medical Center, I was given steroids, multiple pills for infection and my first dose of chemo. The nurse said that this first dose could be highly allergenic to patients. One of the negative reactions of the first bag of chemo is uncontrollable shaking among other reactions. In order for early detection of a patient's tolerance, the IV drip is set to enter the patient's body at a very slow pace. If there is no abnormal reaction, the drip pace is increased until maximum drip is achieved. Praise God, I had no abnormal reactions to the first dose of chemo. Then I was told that I was to receive nausea medication through an IV. After this medication, I was to be given a twenty-four hour IV chemo drip that targeted the malignant cancer that was growing on the left side of my face. At first it seemed that my journey to a treatment regime was extremely slow with multiple options. Now, my treatment pace had quickened with a decisive treatment plan that may or may not work from a medical perspective. The doctor said that if the cancer didn't respond favorably to the current chemo mixture, they would explore other options. I realized again, that from a human point of view, doctors are not able to guarantee an outcome. After the doctor has done his best, he can only wait and see if there are patient side effects and/or the reaction of the cancerous tumor, in my case, to a prescribed treatment. It seemed that my hospital room was filled with uncertainty. The medical terms that the doctors and nurses used were very unfamiliar to me. I smiled and expressed appreciation for their efforts and examinations. Typically there was a certified doctor with four or five students.

Theodore Hughes

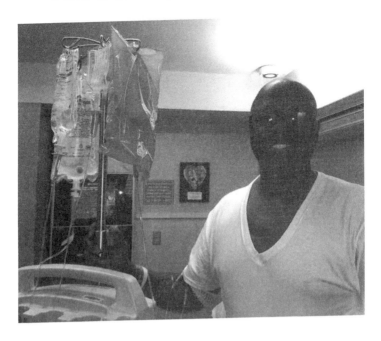

CHAPTER FIVE
Chemo Medications and Side Effects

I was told that the first Chemotherapy medication that I was to receive is called Rituximab, trade name Rituxan, preceeded by five and one half tablets of Prednisone.

Rituxan must be administered very slowly through an IV, while monitoring the patient for allergic reactions. After a few minutes of receiving Rituxan, it was determined that I was not going to have a reaction, so the IV drip was turned to maximum flow. After the Rituxan emptied into my body, the attending nurse placed a bag of Etoposide, Cyclophosphamide, Doxorubicin Hydrochloride, and Vincristine Sulfate on the IV pole, which was to drip to completion over a twenty-four hour period, after which, another five bags of chemo would be hung. This procedure would be repeated throughout my five day stay in the hospital. I received this amount of medication, in this order, for six weeks, with a two week break after each week for my body to recover.

Some allergic reactions associated with the chemo medication I received are:

- skin rash, itching, swelling of the face, lips and tongue, low blood counts, decrease in the number of white blood cells, red blood cells and platelets
- breathing problems
- confusion
- chest pain
- fast, irregular heartbeat
- feeling faint or lightheaded, falls
- mouth sores
- redness, blistering, pealing or loosening of the skin
- stomach pain
- body tremors
- swelling of the ankles, feet or hands
- trouble passing urine or change in the amount of urine
- anxiety
- headache
- loss of appetite
- muscle aches
- nausea
- night sweats
- changes in vision
- pain, tingling, numbness in the hands or feet
- seizures
- vomiting
- loss of appetite

- hair loss
- diarrhea
- nail discoloration or damage
- red or watery eyes
- facial flushing
- heart failure

When I was left alone, I refreshed myself with the Word of God. My refreshing was not to escape the possibility of death, but for grace to maintain a Christlike attitude until God closed the door on this chapter of my life. During this early process, I was told that I would lose all body hair. Because I sported a baldhead, the loss of hair did not move me. When I was told that my fingernails and toenails would die, that grabbed my attention.

The Scriptures principles that I embraced then and now as I was informed of the negative symptoms that occur during my journey to healing are:

Hebrews 11:1 ~ "11 Now faith is the substance of things hoped for, the evidence of things not seen." (NKJV)

Hebrews 11:6 ~ "6 But without faith it is impossible to please Him, for he who comes to God must believe that He is, and that He is a rewarder of those who diligently seek Him." (NKJV)

Joshua 1:8 ~ "8 This Book of the Law shall not depart from your mouth, but you shall meditate in it day and night, that you may observe to do according to all that is written in it. For then you will make your way prosperous, and then you will have good success." (NKJV)

Psalms 61:2 ~ "2 From the end of the earth I will cry to You, When my heart is overwhelmed; Lead me to the rock that is higher than I." (NKJV)

Psalms 18:46 ~ "46 The Lord lives! Blessed be my Rock! Let the God of my salvation be exalted." (NKJV)

Psalms 27:5 ~ "5 For in the time of trouble He shall hide me in His pavilion; In the secret place of His tabernacle He shall hide me; He shall set me high upon a rock." (NKJV)

Psalms 48:14 ~ "14 For this God is our God for ever and ever: he will be our guide even unto death." (KJV)

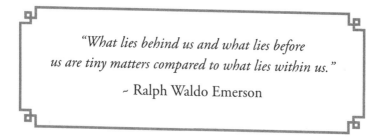

"What lies behind us and what lies before us are tiny matters compared to what lies within us."

~ Ralph Waldo Emerson

The mental battle that I experienced, from the diagnosis until now, was very difficult. **Several thoughts that I wrestle with are**:

1. Is God finished with me?
2. Is this the way I am to die?
3. Do I fight or surrender?
4. Will I recover?
5. What will be the side effects of chemotherapy?

6. Do I retire? If so, will I be able to support my family with Social Security?
7. What will the co-pay medical cost be?
8. Will I be able to communicate how I really feel emotionally?
9. Will I ever be able to help people again?
10. How can I keep my family from the pain of this moment?
11. How disruptive is this to so many people who know me?

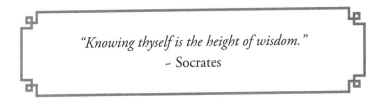

"Knowing thyself is the height of wisdom."
~ Socrates

The kind of cancer that was growing on the left side of my face (Burkitt's Lymphoma) has been discovered to attack the brain and spine.

As a result of this, I underwent a Lumbar Puncture. A lumbar puncture or (spinal tap) is performed in the lower back, in the lumbar region. During a lumbar puncture, a needle is inserted between two vertebrae to remove a sample of the fluid that surrounds the brain and spinal cord. The purpose was to determine if I had cancer of the brain or spinal cord, and to inject an equal amount of Chemo to destroy any cancer cells in my spin or brain fluids.

It was during this time that one of the doctors said, **"The only hope that you have Mr. Hughes is chemotherapy."** I paused. The statement, **"THE ONLY HOPE"** ran counter to my confidence in the power of God. I gave the doctor respect for his tenure as a doctor, medical skills and scientific ability. My response was and continues to be that chemotherapy cannot work without the healing power of God, the stripes of Jesus and the power of the Holy Spirit. As a matter of fact I told the doctor and students present that I trusted God that they knew what they were doing. Further, I said God would do His best and that they should do their best. I refused to allow statements like the one made, pain and inconvenience rob me of the hope that I had in God's ability to journey with me through this process of healing. My mom, Josephine Mildred Hughes, often said, **"God is our healer, He just leaves a little for the doctors to do, because He has given them a goodly amount of knowledge."**

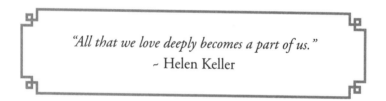

"All that we love deeply becomes a part of us."
~ Helen Keller

After the first week of treatment, the tumor on the left side of my face, softened and began to shrink. I thought that the tumor was a mass that reduced to zero. I later found out that the tumor actually ruptured and the contents emptied inside of my body. I was told that the contents of the tumor would put stress on my internal organs, with the potential of causing infection, organ shutdown or damage. The medication that I was given to protect my internal organs were:

- Allopurinol – a Gout medication, to protect my kidneys
- Fluconazole – Anti-fungal for infection

- Levofloxacin – Antibiotic
- Lisinopril – for high blood pressure
- Metoprolol Succinate – for high blood pressure
- Therapeutic Multivitamins – engineered for cancer patients
- Simvastatin – for high cholesterol
- Tamsulosin – for prostrate health
- Valacyclovir – for the shingles virus

My first week of chemotherapy was without incident. I was discharged for two weeks but required to go to the clinic twice a week for my PICC line dressing to be changed and to receive an injection into the stomach. Neulasta is the name of the medication that was injected into my stomach. Neulasta is a man-made form of a protein that stimulates the growth of white blood cells. The common side effects are:

- sudden or severe pain in your left upper stomach spreading up to the shoulder
- severe dizziness, skin rash
- rapid breathing or feeling short of breath
- signs of infection, such as fever, chills, sore throat, flu symptoms
- easy bruising or bleeding (nosebleeds, bleeding gums)
- loss of appetite
- nausea and vomiting
- mouth sores
- unusual weakness
- hard lump where the injection was given
- bone pain
- pain in arms and legs

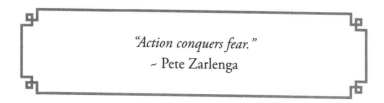

"Action conquers fear."
~ Pete Zarlenga

I am so glad that over the years of reading God's Word, scriptures on HOPE were readily available in my mind. Below are some of the Scriptures that helped me to remain **hopeful.**

Psalms 16:8-9 ~ "8 I have set the Lord always before me: because he is at my right hand, I shall not be moved. 9 Therefore my heart is glad, and my glory rejoiceth: my flesh also shall rest in hope." (KJV)

Psalms 33:18 ~ 'Behold, the eye of the Lord is upon them that fear him, upon them that hope in his mercy;" (KJV)

Psalms 42:5 ~ "5 Why art thou cast down, O my soul? and why art thou disquieted in me? hope thou in God: for I shall yet praise him for the help of his countenance." (KJV)

Psalms 71:14 ~ "14 But I will hope continually, and will yet praise thee more and more." (KJV)

Psalms 119:114 ~ "114 Thou art my hiding place and my shield: I hope in thy word. (KJV)

Lamentations 3:26 ~ 26 It is good that a man should both hope and quietly wait for the salvation of the Lord." (KJV)

Romans 4:16-18 ~ "6 Therefore it is of faith, that it might be by grace; to the end the promise might be sure to all the seed; not to that only which is of the law, but to that also which is of the faith of Abraham; who is the father of us all, 17 (As it is written, I have made thee a father of many nations,) before him whom he believed, even God, who quickeneth the dead, and calleth those things which be not as though they were. 18 Who against hope believed in hope, that he might become the father of many nations; according to that which was spoken, So shall thy seed be." (KJV)

Romans 5:5 ~ "5 Now hope does not disappoint, because the love of God has been poured out in our hearts by the Holy Spirit who was given to us." (NKJV)

I was discharged after one week of treatment, with orders to return within two weeks to start the process all over again and to remember to keep my scheduled clinic appointments at the OU Medical Center. Because I was experiencing dizziness, Michael Murphy, Children's Pastor at Faith Church, drove me home from the hospital. I arrived at OU Medical on Tuesday of the following week for a 9:00AM appointment. Upon arrival, the nurses checked my vitals and drew a vial of blood which was submitted to the laboratory. The purpose was to determine what was needed to bring my blood elements back to normal. Again, a side effect of the chemo is the reduction in blood volume, red and white cell counts. This process lasted for two, sometimes three hour. While I was waiting for the laboratory report,

I was given medication via syringe in my stomach called Neulasta. Again, the shot is an immune system stimulant. The side effect is pain throughout the body and the medicine remains active in the body for approximately three months. I was in so much pain on Tuesday of that week; I got into bed and curled into a fetal position for hours. Throughout the evening and well into Wednesday morning, I felt horrible. Finally, I dressed to go to the Emergency Room. I made it to the living room and sat on the sofa. I was so weak that any movement I made was with great effort. About 4:00AM Wednesday, I was driving to OU Medical Center. There was road construction starting at Mustang road heading east. I encountered a traffic jam. I felt so bad; I exited on Morgan Road and headed to Canadian Valley Hospital in Yukon. The emergency room doctor determined that I had an infection.

Because of a depressed immune system, I was more susceptible to infections than I realized. He determined that the medication that the Oncologist prescribed would eventually get rid of the infection. I returned home at about 5:30AM. I returned to my fetal position and began to praise and magnify God until I fell off to sleep. For the remainder of the week, I could only hold my head up for fifteen minutes. The dizziness was so great that I either returned to bed or lay on the sofa. The physical weakness left me unsure of my ability to walk. Yet, I refused to give into my symptoms. I made my way to my office, which was a mistake. My ability to function and concentrate was very low. I made my way back to my home. I tried to back into the driveway, a procedure that I accomplished routinely. This time I passed out for a few minutes while backing my truck into the driveway. When I came to myself, I had hit the south side of the garage wall, knocked out and cracked some bricks and damaged the garage door. I decided, with the help of others, that I should not be driving at this time. Thank God for Don Bates Jr., who came over and re-bricked the south side of my garage and repaired the garage door supports. Having been in a church service for every week for forty years helping people and suddenly having to stop was agony. Thank God for the call to ministry.

"It is neither wealth nor splendor, but tranquility and occupation, which give happiness." Thomas Jefferson

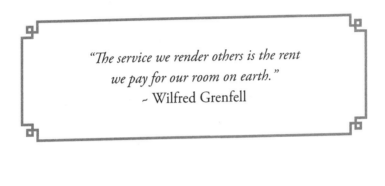

"The service we render others is the rent we pay for our room on earth."
~ Wilfred Grenfell

Theodore Hughes

CHAPTER SIX
My Salvation Testimony

As I lay in bed at home, I began to think about the circumstances that led me to accept Jesus as my personal Savior in the month of June of 1973. I was determined not to just hang around my neighborhood, as I'd seen many young men do. I volunteered to join the military and requested to go to Vietnam one week after graduating from Saint Bernard High School in 1970. As a matter of fact, I turned down an Athletic Scholarship in High Hurdles, because of low self-esteem. I was convinced that I could not make it in college, hence my decision to join the military. When I arrived at the Fort Pork Military Base, I felt a sense of freedom. Because I did not have the restraint of family around me, I began to enter into bad behaviors that my mother would definitely have disapproved. I successfully completed "Boot Camp" and specialized Vietnam Training. I was ordered to Fort Gordon's Military Base, located in Georgia, where I trained in Signal, which entailed communication. When I completed this assignment, my orders were to report to Frankfurt, Germany after a short furlough. Before I left Fort Gordon, I spoke with my First Sergeant, who referred me to the Captain of our Unit. I was not a happy camper. I volunteered for Vietnam and was ordered to Germany. After talking to our Captain with the First Sergeant present, they wanted to know why I was so determined to go to Vietnam. What I did not tell them was that my cousin was killed in Vietnam when the jeep that he was riding in crossed a land mine, which exploded. The funeral service was held for him, and the casket remained closed; it only contained his thumb. It was during this service that I determined not to let anyone do my fighting or die for me. I was asked, "Why do you want to go to Vietnam?" I said to end the war. I was asked, "How are you planning to do that?" I said that I would find the biggest bomb that I could find and pull the pin. I was told that I would be a military risk and ordered to report to Frankfurt, Germany.

> *"Moral courage, the courage of one's convictions, the courage to see things through the eyes of the world is in a constant conspiracy against the brave. It is the age old struggle, the roar of the crowd on one side and the voice of your conscience on the other."*
> ~ Douglas MacArthur

It is amazing how people with bad behavior meet and become friends, buddies, and pals with other individuals with the same traits. Even though I reported to early morning formation and completed my military duties, which eventually netted me a promotion to sergeant, I was a long way from being morally disciplined. During one of our bivouacs, a military encampment made with tents, usually without shelter or protection from enemy fire, I was responsible for establishing communication. I had under my command three, two and one-half ton trucks full of communication equipment and a three-man platoon. Because of our proficiency, communication was up and running within two hours after arriving on site. What I did not realize was that my First Sergeant and Company Commander were fed up with me hanging around troops suspected of dealing and using drugs. During a surprise visit about 9PM, by the First Sergeant, Company command and a Second Lieutenant, in charge of overall communication, I was caught with one can of beer in the communication pod. I was reprimanded, removed from the site and returned to base camp, with explicit orders not to leave the barrack's and to await further orders. About two days after the Company returned from bivouac, I was called into the First Sergeant's office and given an Article 15 of the Uniform Code of Military Justice, which is a non-judicial punishment and refers to certain limited punishment which can be awarded for minor disciplinary offenses by a commanding officer or officer in charge to members of his/her command. I was later told that I was to face a Court Martial because I was charged with drug possession and other stuff on military property. I was told to secure an attorney. Within moments my world became very small. I was provided with a lawyer, who was a Second Lieutenant. He advised me of my rights and told me that I was facing a maximum of five years in military prison.

My mind immediately went to my Mother. She was already a nervous wreck and not well appreciated by my father. I knew that when she heard about my incarceration, it was going to add to her misery. During this journey I was invited to a coffee house on campus, where the Bible was being taught. I told Phil, who invited me, "NO," followed by a rash of expletives. As time drew near for my Court Martial, I decided to go to the Coffee House, which was not far from my barracks. I was ordered not to leave the campus. When I entered the Coffee House, I was greeted by Larry Robinson and Dave Dankirk. I sat on the sofa. I was asked if I had been baptized with the Holy Spirit. I told them in as mean a voice as I could muster, that I had been baptized in the Name of the Father, Son and Holy Spirit. Larry said, "Would you like to go into the back room and pray?" I concluded that they wanted to get me to a secluded room to beat me up. In the seventies, racism was very strong at base camp in Darmstadt, Germany. It was so bad that our Colonel ordered that two blacks were not to walk together except when marching in a platoon or company. I accepted the invitation to go into the prayer room, which was a bathroom minus the toilet, tub and face bowl. I was so frustrated and mean-spirited that I decided, when we entered that room, I was going to punch Dave in the mouth and choke Larry. The unwritten rule was, "if you are going to get beat up, throw the first punch and go for broke." As we walked to the prayer room Larry and Dave were behind me, but close. I crossed the threshold, advanced two or three steps and turned. Larry and Dave were praying in, what I now know as, unknown tongues. Regardless, I was so frustrated and hurt that my Mother was going to be hurt, that game was on. But suddenly something came on me or in me, I don't know which, and I began to speak with other tongues. Then I said words from the book of Revelations, "I am the Alpha and Omega, which is and which is to come, says the Almighty." I yielded, wondering, "What is making me say this?" Larry and Dave prayed even louder. Then I began to cry, something that I was not accustomed to. When things settled, Larry said, "Would you like to pray some more?" With my face buried in my hands, I knelt on the floor. As I cried, it seemed as if my tears were large drops of matter streaming from my eyes. The more I cried, the better I felt. Then I heard a voice that said, "NOW GET UP AND GO." I did not understand what had happened to me. All I knew is that it felt good. Dave and Larry never knew what I had planned. Nor did I know what God had planned. I went back to the barracks, still wondering what I had experienced. Larry and Dave did not explain, but simply rejoiced at what had happened. While sitting on my bunk, I said, "God if you would get me out of this mess, I promise you I will go straight and this time I mean it." A few days later, I headed to a room where a full bird Colonel was the judge and a First Lieutenant was the prosecuting attorney. Setting next to him was the Captain, his key witness against me. The words distressed or distraught do not adequately describe how I was feeling as I considered the seriousness of the moment. I admit that I was guilty of many things but the current charges were not true. All I had was a can of beer. As I sat next to my Second Lieutenant Attorney, his rank compared to the First Lieutenant told me that there was no way I would be acquitted. The Captain was called to the stand. The First Lieutenant laid out the question and the Captain confirmed the accuracy of what he, the First Sergeant and the Communications officer found in my rig. Now it was time for the Second Lieutenant, in whom I had little confidence, to cross examine the Captain.

He asked similar questions but added the words "Are you sure?" the Captain began to lose his train of thought and his lack of ability to speak clearly was very noticeable. The Colonel began to stare at him. After the Second Lieutenant finished, the First Lieutenant tried to get him to re-focus. We are now approaching two hours and both the Colonel and the First Lieutenant were frustrated. The Colonel stopped the proceedings and said to me, "Troop stand up, dismissed." Even though I marched out of the room, I still felt that I was going to be called back. The entire scenario seemed like a dream. I remembered stepping outside into a bright and hot summer day. My first thought was, that I had beat the system. I stopped my prideful self-celebration and remembered what I said to God. "If you get me out of this one, I promise that I will go straight and this time I mean it." I looked toward Heaven and said, "God you kept your word, I promise you I will keep mine." From that moment and further, I am doing my best, with God's help, to live my life in such a way that it pleases Him.

CHAPTER SEVEN
Second Week of Treatment

My two weeks of recuperation from my first week of Chemo seemed very short. Now it was time to return to the hospital. As I waited for Pastor Bates to pick me up, I began to think about the different procedures that I had to repeat and the warmth of the sun, that I soaked in with each breath. I knew that I would be confined to a hospital room for a week before I experienced the rays of the sun again. Pastor Bates arrived about 8:15AM. We drove to the church complex and visited with Pastor Paul and other staff men, who were in the process of setting up our tent for Feeding 5000. After our visit was over, we headed to OU Medical Center. I was assigned a room on the 7th floor after going through the hospital's check-in procedures. I thank God for the many Oncology Nurses that cared for me throughout my hospital stay. Below is a quote that I copied from the public communications board in the hallway of the hospital concerning the sacrifice of nurses.

> *"Nurses are being scorned for being late with medicine and yet they are holding their bladder because they don't have time to use the restroom and starving because they're missed lunch. They're being peed on, puked on, pooped on, bled on, bitten, hit, yelled at and are missing their family while taking care of yours. They may even be crying for you. As you read this, nurses all over the world are saving lives."*
> ~ Unknown

I believe that each Oncology Nurse tried their best to be very kind, helpful, respectful and professional to me. I am so grateful to have been cared for by so kind and dutiful medical care givers. I will always remember their kindness.

As I was being connected to the chemo through my PICC Line threaded under my arm and into my heart. A nurse, who was shadowing another nurse, stated that I did not look like I had cancer. The tumor on the left side of my face had responded to the first week of chemo very well. Thank God, I had not lost any weight and was not nauseated. The lead nurse said that I would have physical side effects from the chemo in the days ahead. I realized that the nurse was speaking from his history of dealing with different patients who responded in various ways to chemotherapy. I began to pray, and say, "Lord, help me to endure and deal with the physical difficulties as I journey to a complete healing from this cancer." I determined within myself that I would not dwell on what may happen to my body but to remain positive and to trust God. The next day before noon a nurse brought in a Spinal Tap Kit. During this second week of treatment, my hands and feet were becoming very discolored, spotty and lifeless in appearance. I began to lose feeling in the ends of my fingers and my feet tingled as if they were starved of adequate blood flow. I brought this to the attention of my Oncology Doctor, who said that this is a side effect of the chemo. I also noticed that I was unable to button my shirt collar and sleeves. My hands and legs became increasingly weak. Regardless of my attempts to use skin lotions, my skin became extremely dry. My calf began to swell and I had difficulty in maintaining my balance at times. It's amazing how a simple task, that was done routinely, became barriers or obstacles to overcome or modify. I have a habit of shaving my head because of balding. But now I noticed that I had complete loss of body hair. During my trips to the OU Medical Center Clinic, I noticed advertising on the office bulletin board, which suggests ways to enhance one's appearance from hair loss. It suggested that hair loss, due to cancer treatment, is a concern for many.

During this hospital stay the doctors were having trouble maintaining my blood pressure and heart rate. Even though I was released to go home and recuperate, I just did not feel like myself. Tuesday night of the next week I went to Canadian Valley Hospital Emergency Room. There the doctor determined that I had contracted an infection. This again was a result of my low immune system. Even though dying was not a topic I discussed with anyone, I was wondering if this was my time to die. When a person's relationships, finances, health and spiritual well-being are in good standing, the thought of dying is not an obvious consideration. But when this good standing is threatened, or by chance taken away, we began to entertain end of life thoughts. I don't consider this process to be abnormal but a deep concern about the reality of life and death. The nurse came into my room carrying a Spinal Tap Kit and said that I was to undergo another spinal procedure. When the doctor, who was in charge of the procedure and medical student with him, entered my room, I was asked if I would allow the student to perform the procedure. I said, "Sure, let him get some practice." I was asked to bend over using my hospital food table as support. As my back was being prepared, the student gave me a verbal, step-by-step accounting of what he was doing or about to do. During this procedure, my wife was setting in a chair just opposite of me. I did my best to focus on her eyes. When he, the student, pushed the needle into my back I could feel the pressure and some pain. The greater pain happened when he hit my vertebrae, which is covered by a thin membrane full of nerves. I moaned several times. As I fixed my eyes on her eyes, I was hoping that this blind procedure or probe for an open area in the vertebrae column would be successful. Finally the student said, "We are in." They begin to extract spinal fluid and replace it with an equal amount of chemo. Then I had to lie on my back for two hours before getting out of bed or risk a severe headache. My wife, Nadine, stayed overnight with me. I was wondering what her thoughts were and how much stress my condition was placing on her. If fact, when I was discharged for my two weeks recuperation time, I asked Nadine, "how are you dealing with all of this?" She said, "If you can deal with it, I can." While home, I wanted to go to church but was told that my immune system was too low to be in crowds. Also, if I had an episode of vomiting, only specially trained nurses were able to clean up the vomit, because it contained chemo. The restriction was to protect me from people and people from me. Thank God for our Live Stream production ministry. This ministry allowed me to indirectly be a part of the worship services.

CHAPTER EIGHT
Third Week of Treatment

When I checked into the OU Medical Center, I promised myself that I would let the doctors know that I had to go to the emergency room for the second time after leaving the hospital. To my surprise I was introduced to a new Oncology Team. I thought that I would keep the same set of doctors until recovery. I concluded that God was giving me a new set of individuals to demonstrate the fruit of the Holy Spirit to. Galatians 5:22-23 "But the fruit of the Holy Spirit is love, joy, peace, longsuffering, kindness, goodness, faithfulness, gentleness, self-control. Against such there is no law." (NKJV) It was a direct reflection of Jesus Christ flowing through my life. I said to myself that this new Medical Team will see my good works and glorify my Father which is in Heaven." (NKJV) I realized later that I was assigned to Doctor Cherry because he is a specialist in Oncology, particularly

Burketts Lymphoma, which is very intense and aggressive. That God allowed me to be under this wonderful doctor for continued care. When I told the doctors about my constant infections, they included an additional antibiotic, which the nurse connected to my chemo IV. I pointed out to the doctors that I had developed spots on my tongue. They said that sores in the mouth are a common side effect of the chemo. I told the doctor that I was not experiencing any pain from the spots, but that they were randomly clustered. For the third time a doctor and a student entered my room to perform a Spinal Tap. This time I was told to lie on my side with my knees drawn up to my chest. After several tries they could not find the soft disc to push the needle through. My level of discomfort was very high. The doctor asked the student to step back. She began to search for the sweet spot to push the needle through but was unsuccessful. The pain was so intense that I was very close to telling the doctor to stop. That is when I began to think about the many people who were praying for me, my wife and children especially. It was during this time that I felt like I was being carried on the prayers of the believers. The pain was so great that I could not focus to pray. I had strong thoughts of telling the doctor that I have had enough, disconnect me from this chemo, I am done. Then I heard the doctor say, "We will discontinue this procedure." I was thinking that the procedure was not going to be re-scheduled. I was wrong. The following day an orderly came in and said that he was ordered to transport me to the Ultra Sound Lab for a Spinal Tap and chemo infusion. My current doctor thought this process was more precise and least painful. This was not the case. Once I was positioned onto another bed, I was told not to move. The ultra sound machine was turned on, and a point of entry was found through my vertebrae. The intern pushed the needle in, which caused me to experience pain running down my left leg. I told him that the pain was increasing. He called for the resident doctor, who was monitoring from another room, and said that I was bleeding out. The resident stopped the student and repositioned the needle and a 15-20 minute procedure was completed in about 10 minutes. This was not my finest hour. I asked the doctor about the pain. He said, "The needle was too close to the nerve." I praised God and told the doctor and student, "Thank you." No matter what I experienced I was determined to represent Jesus in my behavior. I was taken back to my room and told to lie on my back for four hours; the pain lasted longer than that. I was asked by my Oncology Team to tell them about my experience in the Ultra Sound Lab. They were very apologetic. I said, "The Doctor and student were doing their best. I was thankful that the procedure was completed." My tongue had me concerned because it was filling up with flat black spots. One doctor wanted to order a biopsy of my tongue, I refused. Because mentally I was adjusting to my current body changes and did not feel like taking on another challenge. I was given a mouth wash to rinse with if my tongue became sore. I was so glad when it was time for me to go home for two weeks. But before I left the building, I made sure that a prescription for fighting infection was ordered for me to pick up from the pharmacy. When I arrived home I noticed that my food taste had changed. Regardless of what I ate, even familiar foods did not taste the same. It was unreal how my mind held the memory of the food I was looking at, but when I placed it in my mouth the taste and what I remembered did not match.

Theodore Hughes

CHAPTER NINE
Fourth Week of Treatment

When I checked into the OU Medical Center, I looked over the menu and placed an order. Regardless of what I ate, I could not adjust to the taste. I asked the nurse if I could order in a pizza. She said that I had no dietary restrictions. I ordered a medium triple meat pizza. There were two things, among many, that I was told by the doctors; to stay out of bed as much as possible and to eat to maintain strength while in the hospital for treatments. I remember walking up and down the hall of the seventh floor praying for the patients as I passed by their rooms and praising God. I decided to look out of the window near the elevator. What I saw was much unexpected. I saw a man struggling to load a body into a vehicle. Then I heard the words in my head, "that's going to be you fate." The more I looked at the scene below the more uncertain I became concerning my recovery. Another thought came into my head, "You are looking out of the wrong window."

I walked away and went to another window where I could feel the warmth of the sun and see the wonderful signs of life. My focus and praise to God was strengthened. Not long after I had returned to my room, an orderly came in and said that I was to be taken to the Ultra sound lab again for a spinal tap and chemo infusion. As I was being rolled down the hall I saw my Oncology Team doctor, who said she was surprised that I was being taken. Nevertheless, I was wheeled to the lab. The procedure was done by the resident doctor and the pain level was not abnormal. I am blessed to realize the amount of skill that God has given to his physicians. I thanked the doctor and let him know how I appreciated his efforts. Because of the amount of fluids that I was being given, my blood pressure began to rise. The nurse reported this to the doctor in charge and he ordered additional blood pressure medication. I was already being given Lisinopril and Metoprolol to keep my blood pressure in check. The nurse told me that my blood pressure was 190/90. According to the Mayo Clinic Chart on Blood Pressure, the norm is 120/80. After receiving the additional blood pressure medication my heart rate began to increase, which required more medication to bring my heart rate to normal.

1. High blood pressure can cause:
2. Blood vessels to burst in the brain, resulting in a stroke
3. Blood vessels to burst in the eyes causing blurred vision or blindness
4. The heart to work much harder to pump blood
5. Kidney failure

6. Heart pain
7. Heart attack

For the above reasons the doctors had the nurses to check my blood pressure every hour. The doctor said that the high blood pressure was a result of the amount of chemo and other medication that I was receiving. The true answer to correct my ever increasing blood pressure was to disconnect me from the IV drip. This was a consideration but passed on because my 24 hour chemo infusion could not be disrupted. I noticed that my hands, face and feet became puffy from fluid retention. At the end of this hospital stay, I still had an unusually high blood pressure. The doctor said that my blood pressure should come down because I would not receive any more chemo for the next two weeks. The day before I was to be discharged, the nurse said that a bacteria was found in my blood that I contracted from being in the hospital. WOW! This particular bacteria type can cause pneumonia or lodge in the urinary track causing infection. I was told that I could not go home. I was to remain in the hospital for another nine days and go home for two days than return to the hospital. This was a bit much. I was very tired. I asked if there was an alternative. A Home Health Company was contacted. That evening a representative came to my room and explained the program, which my insurance company approved, for IV use in the home. I was discharged from the hospital with specific instructions concerning the need to be timely with my home IV system. I had to attach myself to the home IV machine every eight hours for nine days. I was nearing the end of my chemo treatment and now it seemed that my body was feeling the effects of the chemo and now

I must deal with bacteria. The cause of this bacterium comes from non-sterilized instruments or fecal matter. I began to think about Saul's grandson Mephibosheth. He sustained an injury that was clearly not his fault.

2 Samuel 4:4 "Jonathan, Saul's son, had a son who was lame in his feet. He was five years old when the news about Saul and Jonathan came from Jezreel; and his nurse took him up and fled. And it happened, as she made haste to flee, that he fell and became lame. His name was Mephibosheth."

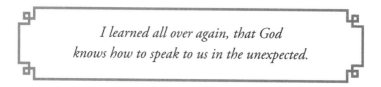

I learned all over again, that God knows how to speak to us in the unexpected.

Norma Officer sent me a card with this note inside of the cover, **"I pray that the chemo is attacking the Cancer and not you."** As I thought about this prayer, I reached out to God with gratitude, gratefulness and said that I refuse to allow the unexpected to change my determination to Praise God throughout my healing journey. (I refuse to lose my Praise) It was during this time that James and Evelyn Travis, dear friends and family members, from Louisiana came to visit. It was so good to see them and to let them witness God's good hand on my life. James asked me, "Are you in any pain?" I was happy to report that I was not in any pain. The major part of my journey was mental. I was undergoing a constant push to not to disdain the various treatments, hospital stays, examinations, checking of my blood pressure, temperature, the struggle to not walk out of the hospital during spinal taps and the ever present possibility of getting some kind of infection. Also, there was no definitive answer if the chemo would be successful. I was told that I must finish the five weeks of chemo with a two week recovery time, followed by further examination before assurances would be given. My personal assurance rested in the will of Almighty God, who has my best interest in mind. Finally the nine days were completed. I had two to get some rest before heading back to the hospital. I used this time to refresh myself in God's word. While lying in bed I had an overwhelming desire to be in God's presence. So much so, that I began to cry. I said over and over again, "God I want to go to heaven, God I want to be with you." As I lay in a fetal position my tears just flowed. Some will think that my coping mechanism was breaking down. Let me remind you that this journey toward a healing helped me to draw closer to the heart of God, not out of the fear of dying but gratitude for the privilege of living life on earth with a purpose.

Theodore Hughes

CHAPTER TEN
Fifth Week of Treatment

I was told by the doctor that I may not need to have another spinal tap because no cancer was found in my spinal fluid. The joy of this moment was short lived when the head of Oncology said that my treatment plan was to have a spinal tap during each hospital stay. Again, I rushed to God in my mind and asked for the strength to endure this procedure with Christian character. When the doctors arrived to perform the procedure, I had to follow the protocol of signing a consent form. The usual statements contained in the form were all of the bad things that can happen, such as spinal infection and possible paralysis. As before, I signed the sheet with confidence in God that everything during this procedure would be successful. I have learned over the years that we should never take anything for granted but to include God in everything.

I continued to struggle with my ability to taste. My wife arranged for different persons to bring food to the hospital, of which I am so grateful. The different seasons made a significant difference in my eating habits. Praise God, I did not lose any weight nor did I have any adverse effects from the chemo. This fact and my attitude captured the attention of many doctors and nurses, who visited my room to confirm what they were hearing. Praise God, which is the objective, that people may see our good works and glorify the Father who is in Heaven. Sometime after twelve noon my blood pressure began to rise. Usually this happens on the fourth and fifth days of my hospital stay. I noticed that my legs and feet began to swell, to the point that I became concerned. Again the doctors said that it was a result of the chemo and saline fluids that I was receiving.

As the nurses were taking my vitals, I noticed that the blood pressure pump reengaged, which means that my blood pressure was high and a retest was initiated. Throughout that night the doctors could not get my blood pressure under control. I was asked if I felt nauseated or light headed. Thank God, I did not. Around 9PM my blood pressure began to drop. My body could have been reacting to the medication that I received earlier to lower my blood pressure. The nurses noticed that my heart rate was dropping. I thought about calling my wife, but decided not to alarm her or my daughters. My starting heart rate at 9PM was 72 beats per minute, which studiedly declined to 42 beats per minute. It was at this time that I felt like I was dying. I said, "If I am about to die, I will go out praying for someone." There was a person across from my room that I could hear mourning loudly. I decided that I would end my days on earth praying for this person. The fatigue that I was feeling was very strange. It seemed as if I could not move but felt drawn to the comfort of my pillow and mattress. I felt like I was sinking or going deep into the mattress. The nurses were back and forth with the doctor, who said that the amount of fluids which I was given maybe a factor. The nurse's orders were to watch me and that the doctor would come to examine me. I was also thinking that my treatment was nearly over and now physically my body was struggling to rebound from the many medications and the chemo. It was during this time I said, **"Lord I have done all that I can to hold on to you. Tonight Lord, I am asking you to hold me."**

I continued to pray for the patient that was moaning and intermittently praise God until I could stay awake no longer. During this time I heard a noise, when I opened my eyes I saw a creature with a long neck, a huge head and a skinny body. From my biblical studies, I recognized this to be a demon from hell. I said, "You need some gym time, get out of here!" After that scenario, **I realized that I was walking around the hospital with my dad**. This is not the first time I have had an out of body experience. When I attended Southwestern Assembly of God College, in Waxahachie, Texas, I was sound asleep and heard my roommate, John Dickman moaning. I looked over to his bed and saw two silhouette-shaped men standing over him. Thinking that our room had been invaded by these men; I jumped up to help John. Suddenly the two silhouette shaped men turned toward me. I began to back up and was stopped by the chest of drawers. I began to pray and the figures walked past me and through the wall. That's when I realized that my body was still lying on the bed. I walked over to myself and set down in my waste area turned and lay down in me. My eyes opened and I roused John, who said that he felt like he was having a heart attack. By daylight John was doing much better. My dad, Walter Hughes, was borne again before he died. He was estranged from my mother for many years. Because of lung cancer and a need of a caregiver, my mother invited my dad to live with her. Because of her love for God, she told my dad that she would care for him throughout his journey. It was during this time that my mom led my dad to a personal relationship with Jesus. Within three months after my dad was baptized in water, he told my mom that she did not need to cook for him anymore. She responded by saying, "Man, I don't mind cooking for you." In hind sight, my mom said that my dad was letting us know that he was nearing death. This was very sad but exemplary. My mom's Christian compassion toward dad changed my life.

At 1:05AM I was awakened to the sound of someone crying. I noticed that it was the night nurse. I asked, "What is wrong?" She continued to cry. I asked, "Why are you crying?" She said, "I am so sorry! I am so sorry! Your chemo drip was to end in 24 hours but it ended in 12 hours, because the drip speed was too fast. The nurse said, "I should have noticed this, because nursing is my ministry." **I talked to the doctor and he said that you have been overdosed**. The doctor said that you will have heart trouble; your bladder will bleed; your liver will bleed and your kidneys will fail. I asked the nurse for her hand and said to her, "You need prayer." After praying for the nurse, I thought about calling my wife but changed my mind. Again I drifted off to sleep. Later on that morning I woke to the prodding of the nurse taking my blood pressure. When the Oncology Team came to examine me, I was told that if my body was not in good shape, I would not have endured the overdose of chemo.

God has been so good to me.

When I was discharged, I was anticipating my final week of treatment. After five weeks of treatment with two weeks of recovery time, I was so ready to finish this part of my journey toward a complete healing. I went to my clinic appointments as scheduled. The nurses, as usual, cleaned my PICC Line and applied a fresh dressing. I noticed that the synthetic tape that was being used caused my skin to itch and blister. I was told that the allergic response that I was experiencing was a direct result of prolonged use of the synthetic tape. I received my Neulasta shot which boosts my immune system. Again, this shot, though effective, causes pain. I noticed that the pain would take place anywhere within my body. The worse area for me was in my upper leg muscles. **Still, I have not lost my Praise.**

Theodore Hughes

CHAPTER ELEVEN
Sixth Week of Treatment

As I was dressing, in preparation to return to the hospital, I noticed that my finger nails and toe nails were extremely thin and brittle. I had to be very careful because they would break at the slightest pressure. This caused me some concern, because I was not sure if my nails would fall off leaving unprotected skin. When I visited with the doctor about my nails, he said that the body has a way of healing itself and that my nails should regrow. After being processed into OU Medical Center, I was looking forward to finishing this leg of my journey to a complete healing. I also was hoping that the doctor would by-pass the Spinal Tap. When the nurse walked in to connect me to the IV, she shared with me the orders from the doctor which included a Spinal Tap. Within two hours of being connected to the IV my blood pressure began rise. For the next four days trying to control my blood pressure would be the concern and challenge of the doctors. The ideal treatment for my blood pressure problem would be to discontinue the chemo. The way I was feeling, I was hoping that they would disconnect the chemo. Mentally I was exhausted. My body was saturated with chemo. My taste, breath and eliminations were inundated with chemo. I lay in bed and watched the last parts of the chemo exit the IV lines and into my body. I called for the nurse to inform her that the IV alarm was activated indicating drip completion. When the nurse disconnected me from the IV for the last time, I was so relieved. I immediately asked for the necessary items to take a decent shower. The doctors prepared a list of medications and instructions to continue at home. Because my weakened immune system, I was instructed to avoid crowds.

If it was necessary for me to attend a large crowd function, I was told to wear a surgical mask. I looked forward to my visit to OU's Clinic. The PICC Line with three heads still dangled from under my right arm. As I entered the clinic, I was so hoping that the PICC Line would be removed. After the nurse had taken my vitals, she changed the PICC Line dressing. I was so hoping that she would remove the line. I was told that the PICC Line has to remain until my Oncology Doctor gave the order for it to be removed. A few days later I was told that the PICC Line had to remain in the event I relapsed. **God has been so good to me.**

During my second visit to the OU's Infusion Clinic I was told that I needed a unit of blood. After about 45 minutes, I was told to be seated in the infusion room of the clinic. The PICC Line that I wanted so desperately to have removed was used to give me a unit of blood. This was the second time that I needed a unit of blood. After having tubes hanging from your body with the endless warnings of potential infection going directly to your heart and the horrible inconvenience of trying sleep without causing a kink in the line, I wanted this line removed. I told the nurses that I did not mine another needle puncture if I needed additional blood. The nurse tried to get in touch with my Oncologist. She told me that she would continue to try and have an answer when I returned. I had become so conditioned to being poked by needles that I ceased to be disturbed when injected. When I arrived at the clinic the following week, the nurse said that my vital counts needed to remain steady or climbing before the PICC Line could be removed, which was vastly improved. **God has been so good to me.** During this week I received a telephone call from the Stephen's Cancer Center, located at 800 NE 10. The nurse said that I have been scheduled for a PET SCAN. This scan would be the third in my journey to a healing. When I arrived at the Stephenson Cancer Center, I was told to sign in and have a seat. About thirty minutes after signing in, a nurse, entering from a hallway door, called my name. I was taken to a small room and asked to sit in a lounge chair. The technician and nurse came in with IV set up equipment. Once the line was inserted blood was taken to determine if my sugar levels were in the normal range. I was injected with a radiation solution, which takes forty-five minutes to defuse throughout my body. Finally it was time to be placed in the PET SCAN machine. I was so hoping that no cancer would be present. After the procedure I dressed and headed back home to wait for the results. After a few days, Doctor Cherry's secretary called and informed me that the PET SCAN did not detect any cancer in my body. **God has been good to me.**

During my conversation with Pastor Bates, I let him know that I was cleared to attend church service again. He requested that an information piece be sent out informing the congregation that I would be returning to church and invited each person to be in attendance to welcome me back. What a wonderful moment! The show of appreciation that God allowed me to remain on this side of heaven for a little while longer still touches me deeply. **God has been so good to me**. When I addressed the congregation, I noticed that I was extremely hoarse. Along with my tears, I felt that I was barely audible. I was so very glad to be back in church. In the days ahead, I noticed that my finger and toe nails were growing back. I had a strange thing happen to me after finishing breakfast and driving over to Kohl's. I began to feel sick to my stomach. I went directly to my truck, thinking if I can just get home and lie down until this feeling passes, I would be alright. As I headed to the exit everything became snow white. I stopped, rubbed my eyes and stretched them as wide as I could but I could not see. Even as I write this portion of my journey to a complete healing, I am still awe struck at the goodness of God. As I sat in the parking lot, still intent on getting home, my sight began to come back. By the time I reached my home, my sight was still improving. I got into bed and wondered if this episode was going to happen again. Today I still praise God that my sight has had no interruption since.

I remember sharing with a Pastor who was determined to resign from his current ministry assignment because of an abundance of difficulties. My words, which I believe came from the heart of God, to him were, "**God knew that you were going to face this kind of opposition.**" Further, "**He knew that you were the best person to handle this**

difficulty." Upon hearing and receiving my words, he called his wife and asked her to tear up his resignation. God, knowing the end from the beginning, knew that I would be diagnosed with a life threatening cancer. Equally so, God knew me. God knew my temperament, attitude and my relationship with Him to endure such a diagnosis. This diagnosis brought me into contact with many very gifted and talented individuals, and I did my best to let Jesus be seen in me. I have learned more clearly about God's loving, kind and intentional actions in the life of His creation.

Theodore Hughes

CHAPTER TWELVE
My Healing Journey is Coming to the End

Currently, I am diagnosed as being cancer free. I still have some chemo side effects in my feet called Neuropathy. Early on, this was highly uncomfortable. The pain was so great that, try as I might, I could not walk at my normal pace. At night my feet sensation was cold and hot. Any contact with the covers only made matters worse. My feet hurt so bad that I had to remove my socks and shoes to rub my feet, hoping to create some sort of relief. Thank God, for His Mercy. I am now only experiencing numbness and discomfort in my big toes. I have some calf swelling, which requires me to wear compression socks. My overall energy has come back. It is so wonderful to be back in the mix of ministry. I have been given the opportunity to preach in every Wednesday night service throughout 2014. Each night I have the opportunity to present stages of my Journey to a healing in a preaching format. Above all, I have been a resource to four individuals in our church who have been diagnosed with different types of cancer. As well as being an encourager to many who are dealing with the tough moments of life. My treatment covered a period of eight months and several PET SCANS. I underwent another PET SCAN August 11, 2014 at the Stephenson Cancer Center in Oklahoma City. I received a telephone call from the nurse who said that Doctor Cherry does not see any more cancer in my body. I am scheduled for another PET SCAN in November 2014. It was during our August 2014 Feeding 5000 outreach and early preparation that I pushed my body. Before this time I was unsure about my body's reaction to the strain and stress of heavy lifting. l am happy to report that God's grace is sufficient and that my body reacted very well. I am so thankful for the many prayers, kind words, and many meals. I could not have gotten through the many difficult procedures and volumes and volumes of chemo without your generous prayer support. Thank you for not giving up on me.

# When A Healing Becomes A Journey

OU Physicians Hematology/Oncology
Stephenson Oklahoma Cancer Ctr 800 NE 10th St, Suite 2500 Oklahoma City, OK 73104
405-271-8299 Fax: 405-271-8490

August 11, 2014
Page 1
Chart Document

THEODORE HUGHES Home: (405)264-7104
Male DOB: 05/07/1951   2459217   Ins: UNITED H (659) Grp: 722266

08/04/2014 - Radiology Reports: - PET/CT TUM SKUL BS MIDTHIGH
Provider: MoHamad Cherry MD
Location of Care: OU Physicians

```
Patient: THEODORE  HUGHES
ID: HCA RAD E002586765
Note: All result statuses are Final unless otherwise noted.

Tests: (1)  - PET/CT TUM SKUL BS MIDTHIGH (TUMSBMT)
1  - PET/CT TUM SKUL BS MIDTHIGH
                    <No Reported Value>
         STEPHENSON OKLAHOMA CANCER CENTER - A SERVICE OF OU MEDICAL CENTER
800 NE 10TH                       PET SCAN                PHONE: (405) 271-4889
Oklahoma City, OK 73104        CONSULTATION REPORT          FAX: (405) 271-4893
-------------------------------------------------------------------------------
LOC/RM: EK.LAB/          PACS ID: E1980301        MRN:       E002586765
PT. TYPE: REG RCR                                         HUGHES,THEODORE
ACCT#: E00647560247            DOB: 05/07/1951 AGE: 63       SEX: M
-------------------------------------------------------------------------------
ORD PROVIDER: Cherry MD, Mohamad          EXAM STARTED: 08/04/14   1000
ATT PROVIDER: Cherry MD, Mohamad          EXAM COMPLETED: 08/04/14  1100
ADMISSION CLINICAL DATA: BURKITT'S LYMPHOMA


EXAMS:                                         CPT:
004118028 PET/CT TUM SKUL BS MIDTHIGH          78815
```

Clinical History: 63-year-old gentleman with diagnosis of Burkitt's lymphoma is status post chemotherapy in August 2013. PET/CT is performed to restage.

Comparison: PET/CT dated 04/08/2014 is compared.

Radiopharmaceutical: 13.9 mCi F-18 fluorodeoxyglucose intravenously.

Technique: Prior to injection of the radiopharmaceutical, the patient's blood glucose is 101 mg/dL. Following injection and a 60 minute distribution interval, noncontrast CT is performed from the mid thigh to the skull vertex for attenuation correction of PET scan and to assist in localizing the PET findings subsequently, PET scan is performed from vertex to mid thigh utilizing bed stops at 3 minutes per stop.

Findings:
Head and neck: The brain demonstrates no definite focal abnormal FDG activity. Oral, pharyngeal, salivary and laryngeal activity appears ordinary. A small right maxillary sinus mucus retention cyst is unchanged, without significant FDG activity on axial image 53. The previously described soft tissue thickening along the left platysma muscle is no longer evident. No hypermetabolic cervical or supraclavicular lymphadenopathy is appreciated.

Chest: No hypermetabolic pulmonary nodules are appreciated. The previously noted inflammatory-appearing changes in the paraspinous right lower lobe are unchanged with SUV of 2.4 today as compared to 2.6 previously. There are adjacent osteophytes on axial image 139. Review of the mediastinum and axillae reveals no hypermetabolic

OU Physicians Hematology/Oncology
Stephenson Oklahoma Cancer Ctr 800 NE 10th St, Suite 2500 Oklahoma City, OK 73104
405-271-8299 Fax: 405-271-8490

August 11, 2014
Page 2
Chart Document

THEODORE HUGHES Home: (405)264-7104
Male DOB: 05/07/1951   2459217   Ins: UNITED H (659) Grp: 722266

lymphadenopathy. Physiologic activity is noted in the myocardium.

Abdomen and pelvis: Normal physiologic activity is noted in the liver, spleen, stomach and bowel. No adrenal hypermetabolism is appreciated. Urinary activity is noted in the kidneys, left ureter, and urinary bladder. No hypermetabolic lymphadenopathy is appreciated below the diaphragm.

Musculoskeletal: No FDG-avid osseous metastases are appreciated. There is physiologic bone marrow and muscle uptake. Again noted is arthritic-appearing activity about the right sternoclavicular joint and left L4/L5 facet joint, unchanged.

Impression:

PAGE 1   Signed Report   (CONTINUED)

```
         STEPHENSON OKLAHOMA CANCER CENTER - A SERVICE OF OU MEDICAL CENTER
800 NE 10TH                         PET SCAN              PHONE: (405) 271-4889
Oklahoma City, OK 73104         CONSULTATION REPORT        FAX: (405) 271-4893
-------------------------------------------------------------------------------
LOC/RM: EK.LAB/            PACS ID: E1980301         MRN:         E002596765
PT. TYPE: REG RCR                                          HUGHES, THEODORE
ACCT#: E00647560247                      DOB: 05/07/1951 AGE: 63     SEX: M
-------------------------------------------------------------------------------
ORD PROVIDER: Cherry MD, Mohamad         EXAM STARTED:   08/04/14    1000
ATT PROVIDER: Cherry MD, Mohamad         EXAM COMPLETED: 08/04/14    1100
ADMISSION CLINICAL DATA: BURKITT'S LYMPHOMA

EXAMS:                                              CPT:
004118028 PET/CT TUM SKUL BS MIDTHIGH               78815
  <Continued>
```

1. Stable exam, without convincing scintigraphic evidence for FDG-avid malignancy.
****
I have viewed the images and/or data and approve the report.

** Electronically Signed by M.D. 131 DALE M. BRANNON **
**   on 08/04/2014 at 1247   **
Reported and signed by: DALE M. BRANNON, M.D.   131